Save with

CLEAN SAFE

"THE COLUCCI COLLECTION"

of economical household cleaning
formulas

compiled by William Colucci
© Copyright 2010
I.S.B.N.
978-0-9866436-1-3

ISBN 978-0-9866436-1-3

90000

9 780986 643613

Index

Please note: The quick links from the index to the formulas does not work with all programs.

i.   **Introduction**

My deepest thank you for beginning and my most earnest request that you proceed to read further. I have carefully compiled this collection from as many reliable sources as I could find and I trust you will find them useful in replacing the marketing gurus rendition of what we should be using to clean our homes.

The concerns which prompted me to compile these formulas are (1) The damage wrought by harsh chemicals used for simple tasks (2) The dangers in the pharmacopoeia of these chemicals found in almost every household and (3) The exorbitant cost associated with maintaining a household laboratory of expensive chemical formulas. Our great grandmothers were as neat and clean a bunch as you would ever want to meet and they did all their cleaning with a few basic ingredients and a lot of enthusiasm. It seems that we have come full circle. Society has tried the miracle cleaners and wonder detergents and our floors don't look any better and our shirts really are no brighter, but our ozone layer has holes in it and our cities are congested with an ever growing haze of smog. The problem of growing pollution has never been truer than today; if we are not part of the solution, we are part of the problem.

Please read through this collection and I hope you
will try these formulas.

1.   **ALL PURPOSE CLEANERS**

Most all purpose cleaners sold in stores contain 80% to 90% water, their effectiveness comes from the very strong caustic agents in them. These chemicals are harmful to your skin and can be dangerous if swallowed. The hierarchy of safety in more natural cleaner varies with their chemical strengths and affects their abilities to get the job done. Generally, try baking soda and/or vinegar first. They is the safest and most versatile cleaners. If these don't work, try washing soda and only graduate to the harsher ammonia when necessary. For the simples cleaning of upholstery and carpets just sprinkle on baking soda, rub it in gently and then spray with 5% vinegar. The bubbling action will pull out many stains. After using several of the methods outlined here, cleaning naturally will become second nature to you and your friends will start asking our advice on cleaning methods. You are already becoming part of the solution.

2.   **AMMONIA (used directly)**

For tough cleaning jobs, such as lipstick, tar and grease stains, apply household ammonia directly to the stain. For regular day to day cleaning use an ammonia based all purpose cleaner.

3.   **AMMONIA BASED ALL PURPOSE CLEANERS**

1/2 cup Household Ammonia
1 gallon warm water

Mix ingredients in a container. Use on any painted or durable surface. Take care of overdoing heavy cleaning on fine wood surfaces. Yields: about 1 gallon

4.   **WASHING SODA HOUSEHOLD CLEANER**

3 tablespoons washing soda
1 quart warm water

Mix thoroughly, with a rag or if necessary a stiff brush apply solution to surface to be cleaned. This formula is particularly effective on heavily soiled items such as broiler pans and barbecue grills. Yields: about 1 quart

5.   **AMMONIA/WASHING SODA CLEANER**

1/2 cup household ammonia
1/2 cup washing soda
1 gallon warm water (not hot)

Mix ingredients thoroughly. Care should be taken to rinse cleaned surfaces thoroughly after use.

NOTE: THIS IS A POWERFUL CLEANER. FOR EFFECTIVE ENVIRONMENTAL AND ANTI-POISONING TACTICS, IT SHOULD BE USED SPARINGLY. THIS MIXTURE IS BETTER THAN SOME STORE BOUGHT PRODUCTS AND EQUAL IN SAFETY TO OTHERS.

6. **BAKING SODA, HOUSEHOLD AMMONIA, WHITE VINEGAR CLEANER**

1/4 cup baking soda
1/2 cup household ammonia
1/2 cup white vinegar
1/2 gallon warm water

Pour all ingredients into a large container and mix thoroughly. Larger or smaller supplies of cleaners can be made by multiplying or dividing the ingredients equally.

For an effective wax stripper, double all ingredients, except water. Remember to rinse all surfaces with clean water and always remember to store unused portions of cleaner solutions in a clean container with a tight fitting top.

7.   VINEGAR BASED GLASS CLEANERS

Mix

- 1/2 cup white vinegar
  1 gallon warm water

    or

- 1/2 cup white vinegar
  1 pint rubbing alcohol
  1 tsp. dishwashing liquid (liquid for hand washing dishes)
  1 gallon water

    or

- (Ammonia based cleaner)
  1/2 cup household ammonia
  1 gallon water

    or

- 1/2 cup ammonia
  1 pint rubbing alcohol
  1 tsp. dishwashing liquid
  1 gallon of water
      or

- 1/2 cup of cornstarch
  2 quarts of warm water

    or

15

- 1 pint cold water
  1 tsp. vinegar

  or

- Wash with pure soap and water, and rinse with vinegar and water.

Apply any of these with old newspaper, (wet the newspaper and squeeze it almost dry) or with a lint free cloth.

NOTE: SPRAY BOTTLES ARE HANDY APPLICATORS BUT ALWAYS REMEMBER TO SPRAY THE CLEANER ON A RAG, NOT ON THE SURFACE TO BE CLEANED.
THIS WILL HELP KEEP THE CLEANER FROM POLLUTING THE ATMOSPHERE AND YOUR LUNGS.

8.   SCRATCH REMOVERS FOR GLASS

To some extent these applications will remove the scratch by polishing down the glass surface. To some extent they make the stain less apparent by removing the coloration within the scratch.

Try them and see which one you like best.

8.1 ABRASIVE SCRATCH REMOVER

2 tbsp. glycerin
2 tbsp. jeweler's rouge (if available)
2 tbsp. water

Mix all ingredients in a small container with a tight fitting lid for intended storage. Apply mixture with a clean cloth, rub well in a small circular motion and changing strokes. Rinse with clean water, repeat as necessary.

or

8.2 SCRATCH/STAIN REMOVER

1 part dry mustard
1 part white vinegar

Blend ingredients well and apply with your finger or a clean toothbrush. Rinse with clean water.

Try cleaning the scratch with toothpaste, the stronger the better (preferably a "whitening" type of toothpaste). Rub the toothpaste into the scratch until it disappears.

9.   DISHWASHING BY HAND

1 pint pure soap (hard bar soap, soap flakes
or soap ends)
1 gallon water

Grate bar soap if necessary, remembering to oil the grater with vegetable oil to facilitate cleaning. Place grated soap or flakes into a pot with water and heat to dissolve the mixture.   Place in an old squirt applicator bottle which will give you all the convenience of a store bought product.

You can also add vinegar to help cut stubborn grease.   Vinegar will also help de-lime kettles, sinks and your humidifiers.

10.   SCOURING   POWDERS   AND CLEANERS

The commercial scouring powders most commonly used today are full of strong substances that wear down the surface being cleaned like fine sandpaper. Such powders often contain feldspars, volcanic ash, silica, clay fillers plus soap or detergent.   Bleach and phosphates are sometimes added as well.

An excellent alternative to these abrasive cleaners for cleaning surfaces that are susceptible to damage is the use of a plastic mesh. Some of the all purpose cleaners included in this book will work as will some hard scrubbing, but nothing replaces "elbow grease".

EASILY SCRATCHED SURFACES

The following surfaces will be scratched by common scouring powders :

- **Formica** surfaces (commonly table or counter tops, even the burn resistant formica surfaces will fade and look dull after many scrubbings with abrasive cleaners).

- **Enameled surfaces** (commonly refrigerators, stoves, bathtubs, bathroom sinks, toilets).

- **Plastic** (some tabletops, microwave ovens).

- Any painted surface.

When a scouring powder is necessary try the following:

10.1 SCOURING CLEANER

1/4 cup soap flakes
2 tsp. borax
1 1/2 cups boiling water
1/4 cup whiting ($CaCO_3$ also called Calcium Carbonate or is recognized as powdered chalk)

Mix soap flakes and borax in boiling water and stir well. Allow to cool and add whiting. This mixture will keep well. Add more whiting to change the texture from mildly abrasive to more abrasive.

10.2   SIMPLE SCOURING POWDER

Make a paste out of baking soda and water and use this paste to scour the surface you are cleaning.

For a little extra cleaning, leave the paste sitting on the soiled surface for twenty minutes before sponging it off. Baking soda will both scour and bleach; as a bonus it will also deodorize.

10.3   HANDY   LEMON   SCOURING PAD

Try sprinkling a little borax on half a lemon and use it for scouring stains. This is a tough scouring pad option and it might damage delicate surfaces.

11.   HINTS FOR CLEANING BURNED POTS AND PANS

- Pour baking soda over the bottom of a burned pot. Let it stand for a couple of hours and the scorched debris should then lift out easily.

- Remove stains from a pan with a non-stick surface by boiling a mixture of water and baking soda in it (1 cup water to 2 tbs. baking soda). Remember to cure the surface of the pan by wiping it lightly with cooking oil before using it again.

- Boil a solution of vinegar and water (1/4 cup vinegar to one quart of water), in a kettle or pot with lime deposits for about 15 minutes. Rinse thoroughly.

- Try using a plastic vegetable bag such as you would get onions or potatoes in for a scrubber. It won't scratch most surfaces and is strong enough for just about all scrubbing jobs.

12 . BAKING SODA SINK CLEANER

Sprinkle baking soda onto a damp cloth; rub this over the stain or mark until it is clean. Used regularly, this method should maintain a clean, stainless sink.

13. BORAX SINK CLEANER

3 tbs. Borax
1 tbs. Lemon juice

21

2 drops household ammonia (optional)

Make a paste of borax and lemon juice and scrub it into the stain with a plastic or nylon scrubber. Add ammonia only as a last resort.

14. STAINLESS STEEL SINK CLEANERS

Most of the ammonia based cleaners listed under ALL PURPOSE CLEANERS at the beginning of this book will work well on stainless steel sinks. To
give your sink an exceptional appearance, rub the clean sink down with a little baby oil or mineral spirits and wipe off excess oil.

15. DRAIN CLEANING

Most commercial drain cleaners contain lye, a chemical that when mixed with water will burn severely. This is, singularly, the most dangerous chemical in a home, capable of injuring or even killing in the most painful way, yet many people store it under their kitchen sink accessible to children. Please avoid this chemical at all costs.

To maintain the drains in your house start with regular maintenance; as explained below.

16.   DRAIN MAINTENANCE

Never pour liquid grease or fat down a drain. If the fat doesn't harden at room temperature, set it in the refrigerator for a few hours then throw it out with the garbage and never, pour coffee grounds or rice down the drain. o keep your drain in peak condition, pour one half cup of baking soda down the drain followed by one half cup of vinegar, followed by 1/8 cup of salt. Do this every week to keep the drains clean.

If the drain is emptying slowly, add to the above recipe, one half cup of washing soda (Sodium Carbonate, available at most grocery stores), wait fifteen minutes and flush with warm water.

If your drain is really plugged up tight, try using a plumber's helper, also known as a plunger. This device works best if the sink is full of water (not to the point where it will spill over though). Place the plunger over the drain in the plugged sink and pump it up and down. If water gurgles up an adjoining sink, this means the clog is deeper down than the junction between the two sinks and may require professional help.

My favorite method of clearing clogged sinks, which I regularly do, is to open the trap (of the sink) under the sink and physically clean out the debris clogging the drain.

There are two types of traps I have seen in my experiences and they are as follows:

The traps on chrome and PVC pipes are usually removable. That is to say a whole section of the drain at the trap can be removed by undoing the pipe ends. This trap can then be cleaned out by hand.

On brass and some PVC traps there is usually a nut at the bottom of the trap that can be removed and the trap cleaned out through the hole there. In either case, remember that even if there is no water in the sink there may still be water in the drain, so place a basin under the trap before opening it up.

NOTE: If someone has already tried a commercial drain cleaner stay away from the drain and call a professional!

If these methods don't correct your drain problem you could rent a "snake" from the local equipment rental shop and force the snake down the drain; however, this could damage the pipes.

Remember to pour baking soda down the drain regularly to keep it smelling fresh.

17. OVEN CLEANERS

Next to drain cleaners, oven cleaners, are the most dangerous chemicals in the home. Please try to avoid them.

Electric elements on stoves and ranges can be extremely hot and can also carry quite a shock, so be very careful to never touch them even with a tool or utensil when the power is on. Don't touch coils with salt, soap, sugar or soda, you could burn them out.

When cleaning the modern oven, (refrigerator, etc.), care must be taken because some areas that you might think are tough enamel are now just painted metal, another reason for avoiding the strong chemicals sold in stores.

If you are already catching all the drippings you can with a second pan or aluminum foil, there are still good methods for cleaning burned on grease. Place about one quarter cup of ammonia in a shallow pan (not aluminum) and add just enough water to cover the bottom of the pan. Heat the oven for about twenty minutes and then turn it off. Place the pan in the oven and leave it overnight. The next day the oven will be easier to clean using baking soda and water. If there is just a small area of the oven to be cleaned, soak a cloth in ammonia and lay it over the spot for an hour or so, clean with baking soda.

For cleaning gas range grills mix a solution of three quarts of water and three tablespoons of washing soda (Sodium Carbonate which is available at most grocery stores). Boil the grills in this solution (in a non-aluminum pan) for about fifteen minutes. Wash the grills off in the sink.

18.   **MICROWAVE OVEN CLEANERS**

Most parts of a microwave oven can be cleaned with a mild cleanser. If there is a build up of grease inside the oven pour twelve drops of lemon juice into one cup of water, boil for fifteen minutes, then wipe the oven clean. To avoid this problem, make sure all who use the microwave remember to cover foods so as to prevent splattering without restricting air flow. (See Microwave Oven manufacturer's directions.)

19.   **REFRIGERATOR   CLEANERS   AND DEODORIZERS**

I'm betting that at least one of these tips on deodorizing your refrigerator will sound familiar to you:

• Take the end off a box of baking soda and set it on a back shelf of the refrigerator. Date the box and change it monthly. The used box of baking soda can go down your kitchen drain to keep it smelling fresh.

- Place a small bowl of charcoal pieces or charcoal briquettes on a shelf in the refrigerator. Wipe up spills in the refrigerator with one of the all purpose cleaners listed earlier in this book or baking soda or vinegar. All will work well, while baking soda and vinegar will leave a nice fresh scent. Some of the multi-purpose cleaners are more effective but are strong smelling.

20.   APPLIANCES

If an all purpose cleaner, as described earlier, is not available, try squirting dishwashing liquid (for hand washing dishes) on the appliance, add a little baking soda and clean away. Either pure soap or the commercial dish soap in the squirt bottle will do the job well. This is a non-abrasive cleaner and works well on appliances, Corning Ware, and sinks.

21.   KITCHEN CABINET AND COUNTER-TOP CLEANERS

The multi-purpose cleaners at the beginning of this book will usually clean day to day grease and messes on counter tops and cabinets, however, if there is a particularly difficult grease buildup, try the following formula. You could also try a

50/50 mixture of vinegar and water for daily maintenance and deodorizing.

21.1 GREASE REMOVER FOR PAINTED CABINETS

1/4 cup baking soda
1 cup household ammonia
1/2 cup white vinegar
1 gallon warm water

To soften hard grease prior to cleaning, press a hot cloth against the grease buildup for a few minutes. Mix the above solution in a large container and scrub down the greasy area. Rinse off with a clean cloth or sponge and wipe cabinets dry.

21.2 GREASE REMOVER FOR OTHER WOODEN CABINETS

1/4 cup deodorized kerosene
1 gallon of water

Mix the kerosene with the water and, with an old cloth, wipe down the cabinets. Wipe down again with clean water and dry.

NOTE: Kerosene is highly flammable. Be careful when handling or storing it. It is also poisonous and I only mention it here because of its usefulness on removing grease from wood.

21.3 REMOVING WHITE SPOTS FROM WOOD FURNITURE TOPS

The white marks are typically caused by someone placing a hot or cold cup or glass on the table. The resulting white marks are from water molecules trapped below the finish. To correct this: 1) Place a clean, color fast cloth over the spot; 2) Heat an iron and then place it over the area for a few second; 3) Repeat as necessary to dissolve the mark. (Make sure the steam function of the iron is off and the iron is not dripping water).

22. TUB, BASIN AND TILE CLEANERS

When buying commercial cleaners you are usually paying premium prices for simple formulas often containing chlorine or another strong chemical that is not necessary.

Chlorine has been called the most dangerous chemical in the home. Mixed with ammonia it creates deadly

chlorine gas. Take care when using chlorine whether bleaching clothes or cleaning spots.

Instead of using powerful bleaches, try cleaning the bathroom tile and fixtures with baking soda and a brush, or vinegar or a baking soda vinegar mixture.

The borax cleaner suggested for porcelain sinks will work equally well on tiles and fixtures in the bathroom. It is repeated here for your convenience.

3 tbs. borax
1 tbs. lemon juice
2 drops household ammonia
(optional)

Mix the borax and lemon juice together and scrub where necessary using a plastic or nylon scrubber (personally, I like to use non-metallic brushes for thorough cleaning). Add the ammonia only if necessary.

23. **GROUT CLEANER**

Grout is the porous material between ceramic tiles, usually found in kitchen and/or bathroom floors and walls. Grout can be attacked by fungi which like to grow where it is warm and moist (just like the typical shower), no matter how clean a house is. Sometimes fungi can be easily removed or contained by regular cleaning with full strength vinegar. When this doesn't do the trick, try one of the following formulas.

23.1   BAKING   SODA   GROUT CLEANER

3 cups baking soda
1 cup warm water

or

23.2   AMMONIA GROUT CLEANER

1   tsp. household ammonia
1/4 cup hydrogen peroxide
3/4 cup water

Mix either of these two grout cleaner recipes together and scrub the grout with a small firm brush. Rinse well with clean water.

24.   TOILET BOWL CLEANERS

Commercial toilet bowl cleaners can be replaced by inexpensive, home made formulas that will do the job as well as the store bought variety and are cheaper and safer.

The common commercial cleaners contain acids (usually hydrochloric acid or sodium bisulfate which turn into sulfuric acid when mixed with water). They also contain detergents, surfactants, and sometimes alkalis, dyes and perfumes. These chemicals can be poisonous and can badly burn your skin. They can be fatal if swallowed.

For most toilet bowl cleaning, use your toilet bowl brush and a few sprinkles of baking soda to clean and deodorize the toilet bowl. You might like to try some full strength white vinegar, which will also clean and deodorize the bowl and clean most simple marks off the tank and rim. The baking soda and vinegar can be used either separately or together.

If your toilet bowl has hard water marks in the bowl, pour in white vinegar and let it sit overnight, this will clean and deodorize the bowl.

If the hard water marks are particularly persistent, empty most of the water out of the bowl by either dipping it out or turn off the valve allowing water into the tank and flushing it a couple of times.
Line the bowl with paper towels and soak the paper towels with vinegar. Keep the paper towels moist by adding more vinegar as necessary. Once the hard water or lime deposits are gone throw the paper towels in the garbage, don't flush them as they will likely clog the toilet.

25.   CLEANERS FOR OTHER BATHROOM SURFACES

The shower curtain can often be cleaned with a good scrubbing with vinegar and if the discoloration is just a build up of soap that should remedy it. If there is a severe layer of mildew on the curtain try scrubbing it with a damp cloth dipped in baking soda. If you feel inclined to use your washing machine to clean the shower curtain try the following recipe:

1/2 cup soap flakes (commercial detergent may be used)
1/2 cup baking soda
1 cup white vinegar
Mineral oil

Fill   the washing machine with warm water, throw in a   couple   of towels to cushion   the shower curtain from the action of the agitator; throw in the shower curtain, add the soap flakes or detergent and the baking soda. Allow the machine to go through the entire wash cycle, add vinegar and a few drops of the mineral oil to the   rinse cycle.   The oil will help to keep shower curtain soft and flexible. Remember to remove the curtain from the machine immediately following the rinse cycle, do not spin or re-rinse the curtain to remove the vinegar. Let it air dry.

26. SHOWER DOOR CLEANING

To clean shower doors use white vinegar full strength; remember to clean the track as well.   Both glass and metal parts should come sparkling clean.

27. SHOWER HEAD CLEANING

- Boil metal shower heads in one half cup white vinegar and one quart of water for fifteen minutes.

- Soak plastic shower heads in a mixture of one pint of white vinegar and one pint of hot water for about one hour.

28. FAUCET AND TAP CLEANING

- Soak a rag in white vinegar and wrap it around faucets or taps with lime or hard water deposits.
  Leave on for about an hour to remove the stain.

29. SHOWER CURTAIN CLEANING

To revitalize plastic shower curtains wash them in the washing machine with one large or two medium size towels, add one cup of vinegar to the rinse cycle and hang to dry.

30.   LAUNDRY CLEANERS

Getting the laundry clean is one the most complicated cleaning jobs in the modern home.   We are assaulted by huge corporations who spend millions of dollars in advertising, telling us that our whites should be whiter and our colors brighter, and that only their product is capable of accomplishing this. I beg to differ.

The basic job of cleaning laundry requires a surfactant, which is any chemical that allows water to act as though it were "wetter", to enter the fibers of the clothes easier and to suspend the dirt and oils so they may rinse off easily. In real laundry soap, the surfactant is the soap itself, whereas in synthetic detergents, the surfactant can be one or more chemical ingredients. The synthetics will often contain bleaches and water builders that will make the water more alkaline so that the surfactants will work more efficiently. They also contain corrosion inhibitors to protect plumbing and perfumes to make it smell better.

All this makes for a very complex chemical soup and one we can do without. The basic functions of this complicated mixture can be duplicated with success by using a few good, natural ingredients.

A point of interest: Chemicals used for the "builders" mentioned earlier are often the phosphates we now hear about shocking the life out of our streams and ponds. A few years ago these were considered to be "safe" chemicals. We must now wonder, what is a safe chemical?

The main disadvantage of using soap instead of synthetic detergents in the wash is that, in hard water conditions, soap will often leave a grayish residue on clothes called "soap curd". Older style wringer washers used to force most of the curd, or soap residue out of the clothes as they pass through the wringer.

Modern, automatic washers spin dry clothes and much of the soap is caught among the fibers of the clothes. The soap curd is not a problem in areas where the water is soft or in homes equipped with a water softener, but in areas with hard water it is best to add a water softener, such as washing soda to the wash.

Before switching from synthetic detergents to soap it is necessary to strip the clothes of any residue of the synthetic soap, this may be accomplished by putting the soap through one wash cycle consisting of hot water and one quarter cup of washing soda.

REMEMBER: NEVER ADD CHLORINE BLEACH TO AMMONIA, SODAS OR VINEGAR

31.   **BASIC AUTOMATIC WASHER SOAP**

1 cup soap flakes or powder
2 to 4 tbs. washing Soda

Use as you would detergent, vary amount of washing soda depending on how hard your water is.

32.   **HAND WASH FORMULA FOR DELICATES**

1/4 cup soap flakes or powder
1 cup water
1/4 cup borax

Blend all ingredients in a saucepan over low heat. Store until needed in a glass container. Use when washing delicates by hand with warm water. Use with cold water for washing wool.

33.   **SPRAY BEFORE WASH**

2 tbs. household ammonia
1 tsp. liquid soap
1 pint of warm water

Mix ingredients thoroughly. Spray on hard to clean areas and let stand about fifteen minutes and then wash as normal.

34. DE-YELLOWING SILKS AND WOOLENS

1 tbs. white vinegar
1 pint water
Mix well, wet articles with solution and wash as normal for the particular material.

35. STARCHING CLOTHES

Make your own spray starch by mixing two tablespoons of cornstarch and one pint of cold water.
Use in a spray bottle and remember to shake the mixture well before using.

36. FABRIC SOFTENERS

36.1 WASH CYCLE SOFTENER
Add one quarter cup of baking soda to the wash cycle in your automatic washer. This will make clothes feel softer and smell fresher.

36.2 RINSE CYCLE SOFTENER
Add one third cup of white vinegar to the rinse cycle in your automatic washer when washing with soap. This will make clothes softer and will help to strip clothes of soap curd.

37. LAUNDRY STAIN REMOVERS

37.1 HEAVY SOILS
Mix up a solution consisting of two tbs. of washing soda and one cup of warm water. Rub heavily soiled area of garment with this solution by hand.

37.2 LIGHTLY SOILED SUITS AND JACKETS
Before there was dry cleaning, our great grandpas still looked good when they put on their suites. Try wetting a sponge or a clean, colour fast cloth and wringing it out almost completely. Wipe down the suit with this cloth and it will bring up the look of the material considerably. Hang the suit in the path of fresh air for a couple of hours, then press with the appropriate iron setting for the material of your suit. So next time, you needn't run to the dry cleaners unless your suit is very dirty.

37.3 SOILED DIAPERS
Fill a bucket with warm water into which you dissolve two tbs. of baking soda. Mix well. In this solution presoak soiled diapers.

37.4   FRUIT AND WINE STAINS
Pour salt or hot water on stain immediately. Soak in milk before washing.

37.5   GREASE
1)   Clean with ammonia and water.
2)   Pour boiling water on stain and clean with dry baking soda.

37.6   INK
Blot with hydrogen peroxide or soak in milk.

37.7   BLOOD
1)   Blot with hydrogen peroxide or soak in milk.

2)   Mix cornstarch with water or talcum powder, allow to dry and brush away.

37.8   COFFEE
Rub stain with egg yolk mixed in warm water.

37.9   CHEWING GUM
Rub or pack with ice until chewing gum is frozen hard. Chip away chewing gum once frozen.

37.10 LIPSTICK
Rub down stained area with shortening or cold cream and wash with washing soda.

37.11 RUST
Wet thoroughly with lemon juice or sour milk, rub with salt, then place in direct sunlight to dry. Wash as normal.

37.12 MILDEW
Wet thoroughly with strong soap and salt, place in direct sunlight. Repeat as often as necessary keeping spots moist.

37.13 SCORCHES
Mix a solution of one cup liquid soap and two quarts of milk, boil the article in this mixture.

37.14. DEODORANT AND ANTIPERSPIRANT STAINS
Rub the stain with white vinegar before washing.

37.15 COLA, WINE AND KETCHUP
These stains can usually be removed from 100% cotton and cotton blends if sponged with undiluted white vinegar as quickly as possible. Wash or dry clean the article as recommended on the label.

38.   **CLEANING AUTOMATIC WASHING MACHINES**

To keep detergent or soap buildup or scaling (the buildup of lime or hard water deposits) from affecting your washing machine run the machine through its full washing cycle once a month adding only one cup of white vinegar to the water. The outside of the machine should be cleaned with the appropriate cleaners as discussed earlier in this book.

39.   **WET MATTRESSES**

Remove sheets and blankets from the bed and sprinkle the mattress with baking soda. Allow to dry for most of a   day and whisk or vacuum off.

40.   **DEODORIZING DIAPER PAILS**

Sprinkle baking soda liberally around the inside of the diaper pail, this will help absorb lingering odors.

41.   **DEODORIZING SHOES**

No need for expensive shoe deodorizers, use baking soda; simply sprinkle the baking soda into the offending shoes at night and empty it out before wearing them the next day.

42.   **HAND CLEANING**

White vinegar will remove both odors and the slick feeling from chlorine bleach from your hands. (If you have sensitive skin or your skin reacts to this tip consult your doctor.)

43.   **ROOM DEODORIZERS AND AIR FRESHENERS**

Growing house plants will naturally reduce odors around the house.

Place a few cloves in a cup of white vinegar and heat it in the microwave oven for a few minutes. Place in the room where you want to remove odors.

At the end of cooking a meal in the oven place a few herbs on the back racks of the oven. This will add a sweet smell to the house.

44.   **WOOD FURNITURE POLISH**

- Dissolve one tsp. of lemon oil in one pint of mineral oil, apply with a clean dry rag.

or

- Polish furniture with mayonnaise and a soft cloth glove.

or

- Mix one part lemon juice with two parts vegetable oil and rub on.

45. POLISHING CLOTH FOR WOOD SURFACES

In a double boiler melt together one quarter cup of paraffin wax and one quarter cup of white vinegar. Soak a clean soft rag in the mixture for one half hour and hang to dry.

46. UPHOLSTERED FURNITURE CLEANER

To remove minor upholstery stains sprinkle furniture with cornstarch. Vacuum up immediately.

47. WOOD FLOOR POLISH

Melt 1/8 of a cup of paraffin wax in a double boiler, add one quart of mineral oil and a few drops of lemon essence. Apply with a rag. Allow to dry and polish.

48. WOOD FLOOR CLEANER AND POLISH

2 tbs. household ammonia
1 pint mineral oil

5 tbs. turpentine
1/2 cup vegetable oil

At room temperature, mix all ingredients thoroughly. To apply, mix one cup of solution to one quart of warm water, apply with a mop in the direction of the wood grain, dry with a clean soft cloth.

49. RESILIENT FLOOR COVERINGS

Resilient floor coverings, such as asphalt, rubber, vinyl and vinyl-asbestos tiles are best cleaned regularly with one of the multi-purpose cleaners described at the beginning of this book.
Ammonia cleaner
Ammonia based all purpose cleaner
Washing soda household cleaner
Ammonia and washing soda cleaner
Baking soda, household ammonia, white vinegar cleaner

50.   NON-RESILIENT FLOOR COVERINGS

Tile floors are easily cleaned with a mixture of one quarter cup of white vinegar to one gallon of water. Simply wipe down the floor regularly with this mixture to keep the floor clean and attractive.

Brick and stone floors, being porous, should not be cleaned with soap. For these floors, use one cup of white vinegar to one gallon of warm water. Scrub floor with a brush using this mixture and rinse with clean water.

Concrete can be cleaned with one of the all purpose cleaners in this book.

51.   CARPETS AND RUGS

To clean and deodorize carpets mix together two parts cornmeal and one part borax. Sprinkle over the carpet, leave for one hour and then vacuum well.

To remove oil or grease spots, cover them with cornstarch for one hour and then sweep it off.
For difficult stains blot repeatedly with vinegar and warm, soapy water.

For red wine spills blot with white wine and warm soapy water.

For deodorizing carpets sprinkle well with baking soda and then vacuum.

For spot cleaning carpets sprinkle baking soda on a wet stain and then pour on a little vinegar. The resulting bubbling action will lift off most spots. Blot repeatedly with a clean, dry, colour fast cloth. You might want to add a little water while blotting to get up the last of the baking soda and water. (Hint: you can always us a "wet vac. type vaccum cleaner to remove moisture.)

52.   **FIREPLACE AND WOODSTOVE CLEANER**

To clean soot and creosote from the fireplace or the hearth, mix together one quart of hot water and one half cup of naphtha soap. Heat the mixture until the soap has dissolved completely and allow to cool. Once the mixture has cooled, add one half pound of powdered pumice and one half cup of ammonia. Mix all ingredients well. Brush this mixture onto the soiled areas of the fireplace and allow it to dry for thirty minutes, then brush off the mixture with a stiff brush and warm water. Remember to rinse thoroughly.

To clean soot and smoke stains off fireplace brick, mix up a solution of one gallon of hot water to one cup of washing soda. Scrub this mixture into the bricks with a brush and wipe clean with paper towels.

53.   BRICK WALL CLEAN UP

If interior brickwork should require a touch up, first wash the brickwork thoroughly, allow to dry and then brush it with a thin coat of boiled linseed oil.

54.   PAINTED WALL CLEANERS

- Crayon markings on painted walls can be removed with baking soda on a wet sponge.

- Try using a white pencil eraser, a piece of stale bread or raw bread dough to remove smudges from painted walls or wall paper.

- If a piece of transparent tape is stuck to the wall, try touching it carefully with the tip of a hot iron. The tape should easily lift off. Or try putting peanut butter of the tape for a few minutes than scraping the tape residue off.

- For grease spots of the walls make a thick paste of cornstarch and water, apply to the grease mark and allow an hour to dry. Brush the powder mixture off. Repeat if necessary.

- To clean the whole wall mix:

  1/2 cup household ammonia
  1/4 cup washing soda
  1/4 cup white vinegar
  1   gallon warm water

  Mix all ingredients thoroughly. Scrub wall as well as dirt buildup dictates. Dry walls after cleaning.

55.   WALLPAPER CLEANERS

- Apply a paste of baking soda and water to (washable) wallpaper, allow to dry and brush off residue.

- Try using plain white bread to clean dirt marks off wallpaper.

- A white pencil eraser will often remove marks from wallpaper just as well as it does from note paper.

- Talcum powder or borax will soak up grease spots on wallpaper, let it set on the wallpaper for about an hour then brush it away.

56.   BRASS CLEANERS

- Use equal parts salt and flour with a little vinegar to polish unlaquered brass.

- Worcestershire sauce will also clean unlaquered brass, apply it with a clean, soft cloth and rinse it off.

57.   BRASS OR COPPER CLEANERS

Clean badly tarnished unlaquered brass or copper by soaking it overnight in a mixture of one tablespoon of salt to one half cup of lemon juice. Tarnish will then wipe away easily.

58.   COPPER CLEANER

A quick way to clean unlaquered copper is to dip half a lemon in salt and scrub the object.

59.   SILVER CLEANERS

CAUTION: ANTIQUING ON SILVER AND SOFTCORE MATERIALS MAY BE DAMAGED BY MANY, (INCLUDING HOMEMADE) CLEANING REMEDIES.

- Toothpaste will clean tarnish off most pieces of silver. Work it into a lather using, of all things, an old tooth brush. Rinse off and dry thoroughly.

- Try polishing silver with a paste of wood ash and water.

60. PEWTER CLEANER

CAUTION: NEVER PUT PEWTER IN THE DISHWASHER SINCE IT HAS A LOW MELTING POINT.

Clean pewter with mild soap and water.

61. CHROME CLEANER

Polish chrome clean with a soft cloth and rubbing alcohol, with ammonia and hot water, or with dry baking soda on a dry cloth.

62. JEWELRY CLEANER

- Polish jewelry with toothpaste and a soft bristled toothbrush. Rinse well and dry.

- Soak jewelry in a mixture of household ammonia and water for a few minutes, rinse, then dry thoroughly.

63. MISCELLANEOUS CLEANERS

63.1 CAR
Keep a squirt bottle of white vinegar in the car to clean the windows quickly and easily.

63.2 OLD BOOKS
Air out old books outside on a sunny day, fan the pages to get the musty smell out of them, sprinkle cornstarch between the pages and brush it off after a few hours. Clean the back and the cover with white bread.

63.3 VASE DISCOLORATION
If vases become discolored from sitting for long periods with water and flowers in them, mix up a solution of two thirds clear tea and one third vinegar, allow the mixture to sit in the vase overnight, then rinse out.

64. CONTROLLING INDOOR PESTS

64.1 ANTS
Squeeze a lemon at the place where the ants enter the house. You can also use bone meal, charcoal, cayenne pepper, damp coffee grounds, chalk or talcum powder.

64.2 COCKROACHES

Plug up all cracks around sinks, bathtubs, baseboards and kitchen shelves to restrict movement of cockroaches. Make a trap by greasing the inside neck of a wide mouthed jar and placing a little stale beer or a raw potato in it.

64.3 FRUIT FLIES

Cut the corner out of a plastic bag and secure it over the neck of a wide mouthed jar containing a little beer. Change the beer as necessary.

64.4 HOUSE FLIES

Close windows on the sunny side of the house to keep flies out. Use sticky fly paper to catch flies or make your own with honey and yellow paper.

64.5 MOTHS

Use camphor (a main ingredient in moth balls) to keep moths away. Trap moths by mixing one part molasses to two parts vinegar and putting the mixture in a yellow container. Change mixture regularly.

64.6 HOUSE PLANT PESTS

Soap and water or a spray of hot peppers in water will rid leaves of pests. Be sure to rinse leaves off after.

64.7   SILVERFISH

Mix borax and honey or borax and sugar, place where silverfish are often seen at entry points to the house.

64.8   SPIDERS

Spiders will leave you alone as soon as the other pests are gone. They won't hang around where there is no food.

64.9   WEEVILS

Weevils are often found in beans and grains. To control them hang small sacks of black pepper in your storage area. A few soap berries for every bushel of stored wheat will also work.

64.10   TICKS AND FLEAS

Wash pets thoroughly with soap and water, dry thoroughly. Make a tea of one half cup of fresh or dried rosemary to one quart of boiling water, steep for twenty minutes, strain, and allow to cool. Spray or sponge this mixture evenly over the pet. Allow to air dry as best possible (dogs and cats, we realize will resist) before allowing pets outside. Do not towel dry.

IMPORTANT TO REMEMBER

DANGER: NEVER USE AMMONIA IN ANY FORMULA OR MIXTURE CONTAINING CHLORINE OR ANY CHLORIDE, DANGEROUS CHLORINE GAS WILL RESULT AND THIS CAN BE EXTREMELY DANGEROUS.

Always read the label on any chemical mixture before using it or adding to it.

Label all mixtures carefully and refer to these labels before using the contents.

www.ingramcontent.com/pod-product-compliance
Lightning Source LLC
Chambersburg PA
CBHW031141270326
41931CB00007B/645